Amy Lo

A Language I Understand

Indigo Dreams Publishing

First Edition: A Language I Understand
First published in Great Britain in 2021 by:
Indigo Dreams Publishing
24, Forest Houses
Cookworthy Moor
Halwill
Beaworthy
Devon
EX21 5UU

www.indigodreams.co.uk

Amy Louise Wyatt has asserted her right under the Copyright, Designs and Patents Act 1988 to be identified as the author of this work.
© Amy Louise Wyatt

ISBN 978-1-912876-44-0

British Library Cataloguing in Publication Data. A CIP record for this book can be obtained from the British Library.

This book is sold subject to the condition that it shall not, by way of trade or otherwise, be lent, re-sold, hired out, or otherwise circulated without the author's and publisher's prior consent in any form of binding or cover other than that in which it is published and without a similar condition including this condition being imposed on the subsequent purchaser.

Designed and typeset in Palatino Linotype by Indigo Dreams.
Cover artwork by Jane Burns.
Printed and bound in Great Britain by 4edge Ltd.

Papers used by Indigo Dreams are recyclable products made from wood grown in sustainable forests following the guidance of the Forest Stewardship Council.

For Paul, Owen, Sorcha and Alice.

Acknowledgements

Miniature was first published by Allegro Poetry. An earlier version of *Gran's Dresser* was published by Boyne Berries. *Digging Potatoes at Crawfordsburn* and *Muse* were published by FourxFour. *Paragon* was published by Spontaneity. *Dark Christmas, Gold DMs, Sands of Time* and *The Botanist* were published by Dodging the Rain. *Lose the Light* was published by Cold Coffee Stand. *Memory Box was* published by The Honest Ulsterman. *Northern Hearts* was published by A New Ulster. An earlier version of *Daucus Carota* and *Telescopes* were published in CAP Anthology 2018 and 2020.

Today's Lunchtime Confession won the inaugural 2019 Poetrygram Prize. *Lemons* was shortlisted for The Seamus Heaney Award for New Writing 2018 and nominated for Best of the Net 2020. *Bugibba, 1984* was shortlisted for The Seamus Heaney Award for New Writing 2020. *Opening to the Light* was shortlisted in the Demspey and Windle Poetry Day Competition 2019. *Sky Piece* and *My Granny's Budgies* were longlisted for The Seamus Heaney Award for New Writing, 2019 and 2020.

Special thanks to Gaynor Kane, Ross Thompson, Moyra Donaldson and Trish Bennett for their invaluable support, advice and friendship as I put this pamphlet together. Gratitude to all of my friends, both inside and outside of the writing community, for their inspiration and encouragement. Thank you to the many journals and anthologies that have published my work throughout the past few years and to the Irish Writer's Centre for the opportunity of mentorship with Moyra Donaldson. Endless thanks go out to my family for putting up with me every step of the way. And finally, I want to show my appreciation to my fabulous publishers, Ronnie and Dawn, at Indigo Dreams for this opportunity.

CONTENTS

Miniature	9
Gran's Dresser	10
Memory Box	11
Folding Sheets	12
Daucus Carota	14
My Granny's Budgies	15
A Language I Understand	16
Lemons	18
Bugibba, 1984	19
Dark Christmas	20
Muse	21
Digging Potatoes in Crawfordsburn	22
Lose the Light	23
Planets	24
Lunar	25
Paragon	26
Today's Lunchtime Confession	27
Gold D.M.s	28
Sands of time	29
Northern Hearts	30
Martial Arts	31
Sky Piece	32
Telescopes	33
Opening to the Light	34

A Language I Understand

Miniature

In the beginning, they bought me things
with pedals. Things to move me from my spot.
When all I wanted was a world in miniature
that was mine, that I could hold at once
in two small hands. You see, a book could
take me further than a bike; could take me
miles in seconds without fear of reprimand.

Henceforth, they bought me things with pages.
Things to move me all at once to empathetic
tears; to envy and to love; to anger and to fear.

And in this world of miniature I travelled
through the pages; held my breath on top
of man-made mountains built with words.
Perished in the loneliness of every final page.
Then, breathed myself alive with each new spine
cracked open like a new born dragon sent to
set the world in miniature within my hands afire.

Gran's Dresser

The mouths of drawers were hungry. They had eaten
so many things that no one needed. But children

found use for the mouthfuls of curious that dresser
ate up. Emptied contents onto spare room rug.

Found layers of coins. Ships sailing on a sea of forks.
And silver spoons, inverted moons, tarnished neglect.

Beads. Tangles of glossy knots; years of wrapping
themselves in each other until nothing alone.

Thimbles. Too many for fingers. Ladies in skirts
graced surface of things too fine to offer protection –

for nothing can stop a needle piercing warm soft flesh.
Not even treasured memories of childhood play.

Memory Box

Ineffable: the way we feel.

I file her nails. Dust clouds signal that which can't be said.
Lacquer seals bond onto tip; shines over, hardens up.

But all she knows is shadow from the past;
half stopped to tenderly say *hi*,
touching hands that stroked soft curls, once.

Curl cut; kept in memory box.
Ironic now to say, *remember that?*

For she no longer can give my love a name.

Folding Sheets

Oh God, she loved corners.
Sundays saw her iron out sins from our week.

Preparing them to rest, we stood sheet apart –
huge triangles of cloth squared like envelopes.

Take a blue thing, fold it so it cannot know.
Even in the dark, it wraps itself around those it loves.

Now – safe, and set in pale stone of this moon,
head in crook of arm, you are corner to my cloth.

The Botanist

Here, the scene from some botanical lab.
You as botanist: your kitchen window

sparks our Holocene age; makes glaciers
retreat from warmth of new sun spilt on sill.

Your busy hands propagate, prune, liberate.
Digits mossed and soiled; you birth spider

plants in Black Bush tumblers; strange test tube flowers
whose name you now forget, were smuggled home

from Portugal in ninety-three. This petri
dish prepared for last year's Amaryllis,

is moist and ready to infuse with life.
Everything in jam jars grows. Bursts forth.

Those once clipped, now, more whole since the cut.
Oh, how I want to tread the water too.

To feel my legs like shoots spread out and stretch
my history taciturn into

a fluid womb. Then ink-bled veins touch glass
and it is time to plant. You carry me

with those you grew, on tissue. Attach us
all as brand new beings to the earth.

Daucus Carota

My granny only tailed before she peeled
because you need the stump of leaves to hold
an orange inmate captive while you skin her.

The topping of a carrot's always last.

You behead *Daucus Carota* only when
the final ribbon of her sullied skin
has slithered off.

Then dice her into dancing suns.

Upon the board she looks like agate sliced;
at times she's sceptres; half stars.

She'll dance again amid the broth.

The sun comes up within the pot.

My Granny's Budgies

I remember the bites more than the birds.
Those hooked beaks.

Birds caged so long
they didn't understand their wings.

They couldn't fly.
They wouldn't sing.

Rigid bodies like angry missiles.

I wonder at the purpose
of keeping birds that never fly.

Essence trapped in feathers
of downy dead-still wings.

If I, a budgie in a cage,
sensed the air through bars,
and saw this space

and felt desire to fly –
to topple heights,
to be a flash of colour in the sky –

I too would thrust the only part of me
that fits through those thin shafts

to rip and hook and bite the flesh
from anything

that moves in the expanse.

A Language I Understand

On the Lord's day we ate ice cream
after we went in peace.

The Sabbath was vanilla pod and tendrils
of gold sun, spun like sugar

from the glasses stained in temples
of our God's almighty cliché.

The pews were hard, the cone was soft.
Maybe built with brimstone;

maybe left in air too long. It's hard to know
in a world of inside outs.

With Holy Spirit raised on tongues in a language
only he will understand;

the rest of us are vessels open to the respite
of a day that will be tinged

with guilt because we cannot rest. Maybe only God
can rest in peace,

for making milky ways and worlds and those who feel
both love and guilt,

deserves a break. Quite often now I go to pieces
on the Sabbath day.

The dam of septico about to burst; to spill my fears
into a new-born week.

Take me back to worship my vanilla God, pushed inside the hollow of a cone;

raised in a language I understand, spoken with a cold and holy tongue.

Lemons

I have been sucking on lemons since I was four,
then sliced thin and tinted with gin, my gran would swish
the slice from her highball and bequeath me a slurp.
A young hedonist in love with a sour thing,
I had been preparing all my days for a challenge.

Recklessly, at fourteen, I ate a lemon whole.
Fluorescent caustic bulb: I bit deeply through its
waxy lizard skin en route to *Old Gramp's* house.
I crunched up, squirming with cramps; clutching myself
as the bus left Great Victoria Station, best friend

looking at me with bewildered eyes. At fourteen,
there's no pithy distinction between pleasure and pain.
Besides, I *still* go fishing for yellow moons: I plunge
bare fingers into every drink; letting the lemon discover
the cuts that have remained unnoticed until now.

Bugibba, 1984

and my Granda reaching
for the unreachable branch.

The flower he is picking is for me –
a white peony, open and awake.

Fighting through dark leaves
to reach a halo of bright flowers

he is heavenward –
tiptoed; stretching body

through spacetime, reaching
for the Olympus moon.

I am buggy-bound, curly-haired, entitled.
Observing him, anthropic.

If I asked, he would reach
into the black,

unhook the rings of Saturn
to place around my neck.

Always. He is balancing.
Spanning the gap,

plucking white peonies –
promising to love me.

Dark Christmas

Your last Christmas and we knew it.
You unwrapped six craft ales –

I knew they were too much;
even a sip now gave you heartburn.

Yet you smiled; feigned they
wouldn't last long. But there they sat –

January kicked us in the stomach
when you zoned out one afternoon

never to return; one-way ticket
to the heavens and craft beers

gathering white dust on the floor.
Looking through the old lens

pointed at dark Christmas of my past;
we are starlit; planetary wraiths

orbiting each other. Some day,
corporeal, we'll drain those bottles dry.

Muse

I spoke in words I'd heard my mother use –
that until now had not been mine to claim.

The twenty-seventh day delights in flame
singed by the boiled first breath.

My muse,
my little muse.
You cried a womb-won battle cry
and fell upon my side
still tied; battle scarred; wrinkling into life.
We won, we won. We won just one.

Your face was mine. Yet yours. Yet his.

Can a babe translate the language
of those who chose him without knowing?

Cast off,
cast on – we dropped a stitch and you are this.

You speak in words my mother heard me use –
you claimed my spot and I claimed hers, my muse.

Digging Potatoes in Crawfordsburn

You earned it well, for hard you'd worked;
oft sprung back by the heave of unrooted spud
finding foot in the fertile field of dirt,
you pocketed your time; covered in mud
returned to Cootehall Road to wash away
the sixpence of labour you had endured.

The bath already run by Gran, to say
she knew you toiled the farmer's field for her –
her appreciation: a boiling tub
and hearty stew made from the duggen stones.
Yet, Henry – he earned twice amount in mud
and you sliced half; but every stew has bones

and every day begins beneath the ground
and we shall dig, until every stone is found.

Lose the Light

For the umpteenth time she bellowed *do not
swing those eggs!* At eight a bag of precious

freight seemed to somehow only slow me
down for half a minute. I'd stop that bag mid-

flight; control it like a drone; hover it
like dragonfly on pond. Then something

snapped and once again it swung like on
a catapult controlled by tiny men.

My angry mum, exasperated much,
would state some rhetoric like *how many*

times do you have to be told? and I would
not have liked to be the one to count.

Yet to this day I catch myself mid-swing.
My mother's voice still resonates within the shells

of one full box of precious dozen eggs.
For years I've longed to still defy her words

and swing them high with wild release.
But in the end, I could not bring myself

to peer inside that box and see one cracked;
and know that she was right; and know that life

is short; and find that one fine line can cause
the darkness to seep in and lose the light.

Planets

I felt too deeply.
So, they wrapped me in in the ether.

Each day, reached large and desperate
into endless black;
plucked a world, pressed it to my lips.

Took new planets into me;
gave them my sadness.

Friend, even in emptiness of space,
don't lose hope,
for we can find a home for what's been lost.

Lunar

The ancients placed moonstones
in their mouths to see their futures;
under full moon, energy pulled
inwards, born from their mother's rays.

To see my future, I placed a full moon
on my tongue; yearned to be lunar;
to see what ancients saw. Worship
Artemis; marbleised, translucent;

let adularescence make me believe
that life is moonlight on calm water;
that I am only a spectre dreamt
by Luna in her long pale sleep.

Paragon

I wanted to know I had a body –
for no body is eternal.

As child, the Canon taught me how
to count on fingers of one hand.
In this way, I was fifth –
for he counted in order of who to love.

God, a mighty thumb, bulbous and worthy.
Family, an index less important than God.
Friends, an equator running the hand.
I kept my ring finger for those I did not know.

Then me. Tiniest, least significant, furthest from God.
The most unlike the thumb. In every way.

Now an adult, the Canon's teachings
make a paragon of my hand.

Still, in the night

I find myself unable to love my body.

Today's Lunchtime Confession

I was dishonest for eleven years.
Skimmed my lunch like a stone
into a bin at the door of my classroom;

told my mum I'd eaten every bite;
looked her in the eye, didn't turn red.

Unsure of why I wanted to go hungry
I still feel fizzy water in my gut,
beating wings never fully formed —

belly full of chrysalides; shot full
of holes by wriggling bullets of doom.

But thrill of hunger, rapidness
of heart in throat, like drill,
made me a trilling bird perched at the apex.

When we're close to losing our chains,
freedom comes at a cost. Today at noon

I snuck a sandwich from my bag;
held it up; felt my gut pop. Knew I must
fill up, leave no room for imagoes to grow.

Gold D.M.s

I'm reminded of those gold D.M.s
I used to own to stomp the way
through my impromptu, potholed teens.

Bought gilded at thirteen, the jerky
movements of unsettled feet;
my shuffling caused great scuffing
that needed now concealed.

My Granda was good with cars;
actually, more the cover-up
of things – like accidents. He knew
paint, he knew how to hide faults.

So, he made it his mission to track
me down gold spray that matched
those gilded boots exactly to a tee.

Eventually. Three weeks from setting out,
he called to say he'd found the gold;
my defects were to disappear.
We masked them off, made edges clean;

then sprayed the hissing liquid gilt
like Satan's song; his wealth
displayed in running glittered tears
upon the surface of my D.M. boots.

Still now, I wish I wore my sins
upon my feet; hidden from my heart;
kept close to ground; panning for gold.

Sands of time

In Comber I first saw the sands of Greece,
of Mexico, Bermuda and Iran.

In nine short miles I travelled half the world;
and saw the gradients of every beach

from black to gold. In glass I held those
particles who'd kissed the sea goodnight

beneath the moon's dark pull. Twenty tiny
bottles filled with sand; corked in miniature

to keep the sea-smell fresh. I longed to pull
their corks; inhale the sea into my lungs;

into my very core. Infuse their waters
with my blood; grow scales upon my skin;

swim off in the azure. These were the sands
of time; of days spent travelling the globe

to capture gold dust at the sea in jars.
Each one an hourglass never to be turned.

For time is nothing but a label placed
on life, which cannot be contained in glass.

Oh, how I long to step upon those shores
and pour each bottle back into the earth.

Return each grain unto its rightful home.
Return each grain unto its place of birth.

Northern Hearts

Connolly Station: a surge of passengers ready to forge
their southern paths. As we worked ourselves loose
from the frenzied threads on a free street map we misplaced
our bearings. Dublin had us tangled in her knot
of streets, four feet teetering on convulsing cobbled paths,
St Patrick's snakes bore us on their patchy backs.

Youths with legs outstretched played social in
some skulking alley; hidden from the outstretched arms
of the bustling maiden and her heady throng deeply
drunk on black. Men in bags with cups and heaven-pointed
eyes, brought forth that *blessed are the poor for they
will inherit the kingdom,* and we are all at once consoled.

We spilled into a bar. Fell under the spell of a fiery fiddler
with a stamping foot, a sense of fun and an upturned hat
for half-cut tippers with clinking change. Met Ballymena
man, who border crossed to greener grass, shared stories
into the early hours and hankered for a northern bond.

At three a.m. we laid our heads in attic bed. We clambered
through a laddered window in the roof to find our rest.
Awoke next morning to the *clip clop* of horses' hooves
on the cobblestones of a hectic day, and streamed Irish light
through the curtain crack charging our northern hearts.

Martial Arts

I bring him here to learn discipline.
As we arrive late, shoes kicked off,
mad dash to the mats, I hope this
pays off for him. Hope he isn't me,
five, maybe fifteen, giggly, full
of nerves, unable to concentrate
in class; boiling in a jumper, pulling
at a tight top buttoned shirt,
hoping the day away until we do
something I enjoy. But he is not me.

It is the numbers in him that come
alive when they are multiplied,
subtracted, divided; it is the logic
of finding answers that we know.

For me, these things made me
fidget, wiggle, fudge up. But my
mind steadied at the colours
licked up by the tip of a brush,
the way a line didn't have to
hold its contents; the very fact
I never knew the outcome.

Take the child out of me.
Not much has changed. I am
undisciplined, perpetually late,
horrified by order. But chaos
and logic are mother and son.

Sky Piece

As if cats are typing, weeds grow underground.
In bygone days, our baby took priority –
we stayed up late; everything was tardy.

We bestowed majesty; he threw his hands
from his crib, stole pieces of the sky.
This was our puzzle, sprawling in the nest –

causing eggs to crack; letting winged things free.
We wanted to collect each shard of shell –
reach the end of his alphabet; draw prizes

from the depth of my womb. But weeds
had grown underground, and even the love
we had stowed away, wasn't enough.

Telescopes

We used to love all night –
earth dispersed in space
and supernovas …

We'd take telescopes,
search each other for shooting stars.

Momentum of one heavenly
body orbiting another –

we were galactic, cosmological,
space-shifting the planet-scape;

I was so high, ungravitational;
you – moonish, elementary.

These days, earth reconstructed,
telescopes dismantled,

I search your eyes
for infinite regress.

No first cause; no big bang –
yet still,
traces of those shooting stars.

Opening to the Light

I am in the garden and he is telling me
to go easy on the gin, for I can't hold my drink.

But the sun is shining. And it has been a long time
since I have seen the flowers open themselves

to the light like they do now, and I want to take it in.
He is telling me to go easy, for in the next room

our cat is dying. My beautiful boy is dying.
But the pots are alive with bees and I can hear

the children next door laughing; the neighbour
is mowing, for the rain is to come tomorrow.

The cat could be dead tomorrow he says.
But it doesn't make me go easy on the gin.

For I am thirty-seven and almost everything
I have loved has died. It has been a long time

since I have seen the flowers open themselves
to the light, as they do now. I want to take it in.

Indigo Dreams Publishing Ltd
24, Forest Houses
Cookworthy Moor
Halwill
Beaworthy
Devon
EX21 5UU
www.indigodreams.co.uk